Deltas

by Kimberly M. Hutmacher

Consulting Editor: Gail Saunders-Smith, PhD

Consultant: Nikki Strong, PhD
St. Anthony Falls Laboratory
University of Minnesota

CAPSTONE PRESS
a capstone imprint

Pebble Plus is published by Capstone Press,
151 Good Counsel Drive, P.O. Box 669, Mankato, Minnesota 56002.
www.capstonepub.com

 Books published by Capstone Press are manufactured with paper
containing at least 10 percent post-consumer waste.

Library of Congress Cataloging-in-Publication Data
Hutmacher, Kimberly.
  Deltas / by Kimberly M. Hutmacher.
    p. cm. — (Pebble plus. Natural wonders)
  Includes bibliographical references and index.
  Summary: "Simple text and photographs explain how deltas form and types of deltas"—Provided by publisher.
  ISBN 978-1-4296-5322-0 (library binding)
  ISBN 979-1-4296-6220-8 (paperback)
  1. Deltas. I. Title. II. Series.
  GB591.H88 2011
  551.45'6—dc22   2010029078

Editorial Credits
Gillia Olson, editor; Heidi Thompson, designer; Eric Manske, production specialist

Photo Credits
Alamy/blickwinkel, 7
Corbis/Francesco Muntada, 19
Earth Sciences and Image Analysis Laboratory, NASA Johnson Space Center, 11
Getty Images Inc./Mangiwau, 5
Shutterstock/Jonathan Larsen, 21; Sander van der Werf, 1
Super Stock Inc./Science Faction, 15; SuperStock, 17
Visuals Unlimited/Marli Miller, 9; NSIL/G.R. "Dick" Roberts, cover, 13

Note to Parents and Teachers

The Natural Wonders series supports national geography standards related to the physical and
human characteristics of places. This book describes and illustrates deltas. The images support
early readers in understanding the text. The repetition of words and phrases helps early readers
learn new words. This book also introduces early readers to subject-specific vocabulary words,
which are defined in the Glossary section. Early readers may need assistance to read some
words and to use the Table of Contents, Glossary, Read More, Internet Sites, and Index sections
of the book.

Printed in the United States of America in North Mankato, Minnesota.
092010   005933CGS11

Table of Contents

How Deltas Form

Some rivers rush. Others creep.

They all carry small pieces

of clay, silt, and sand.

These small pieces of rock

are called sediment.

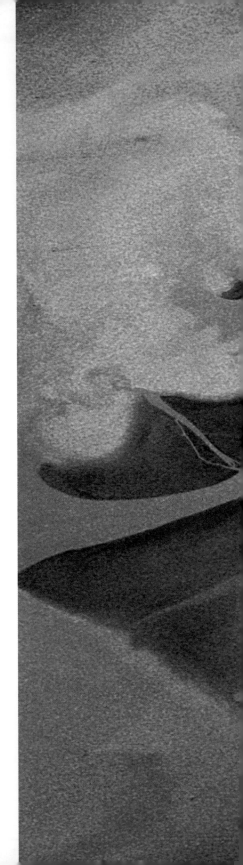

river

Rivers drop the sediment where they meet a lake or an ocean. Over time, sediment can build up. It forms a piece of land called a delta.

delta

Shapes of Deltas

Bird's foot deltas form

when a strong river flows

into a calm sea.

These deltas branch out

like bird toes.

Cuspate deltas form when

slow rivers meet strong waves.

The waves push most sediment

to the sides of a river's mouth.

A pointy tooth shape forms.

Say it like this: KUHS-payt

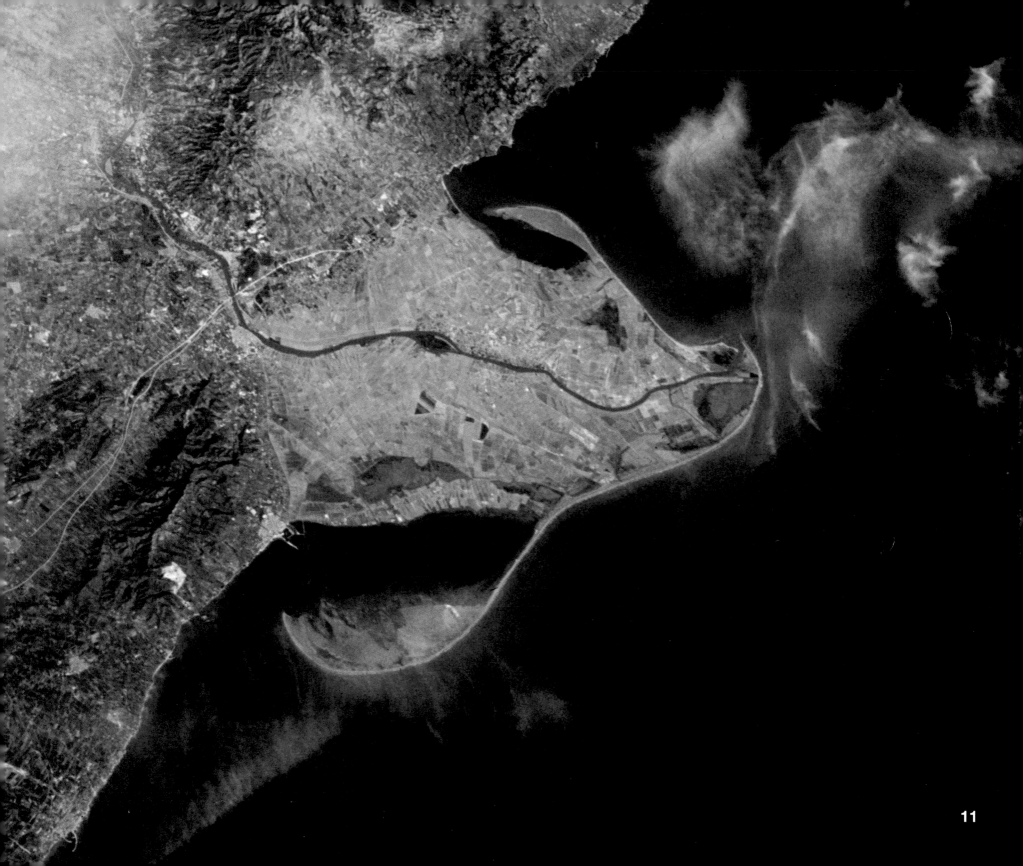

11

Sometimes the river

and ocean waves are

both weak or both strong.

Then arcuate deltas can form.

They are shaped like triangles.

Say it like this: AR-kyuh-wuht

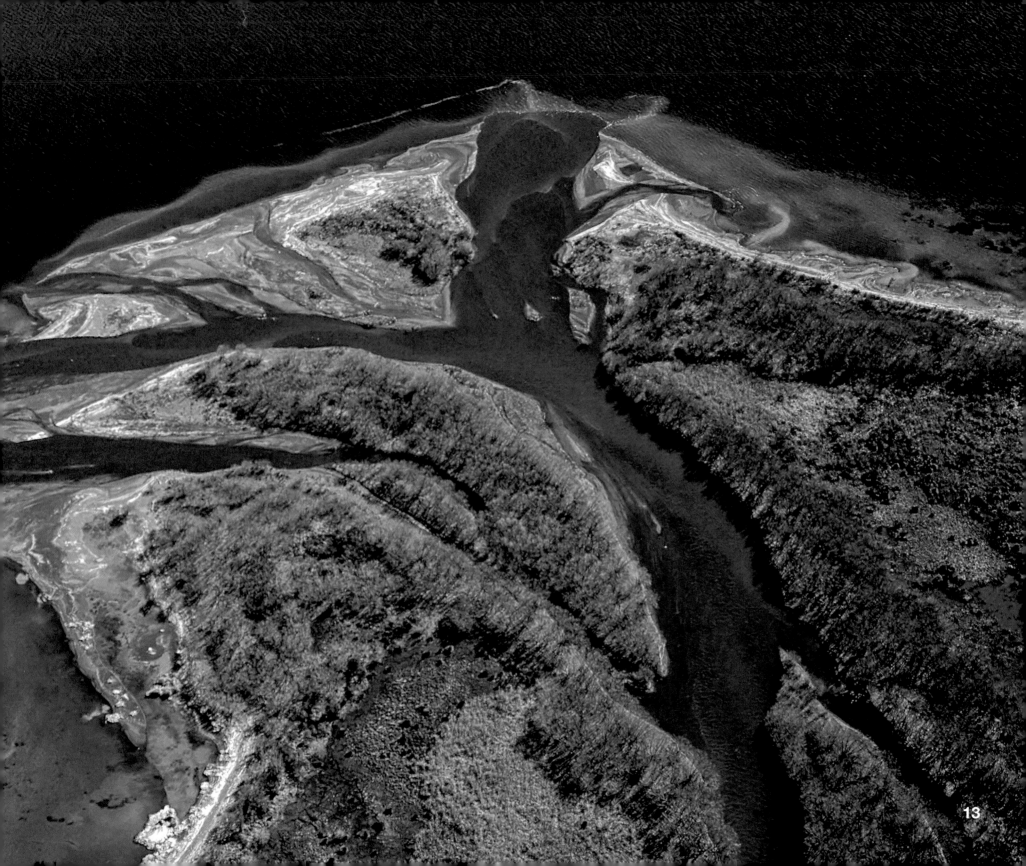

13

Famous Deltas

The Ganges-Brahmaputra Delta

is the world's largest.

It lies off the coasts of India

and Bangladesh. It is 220 miles

(354 kilometers) wide.

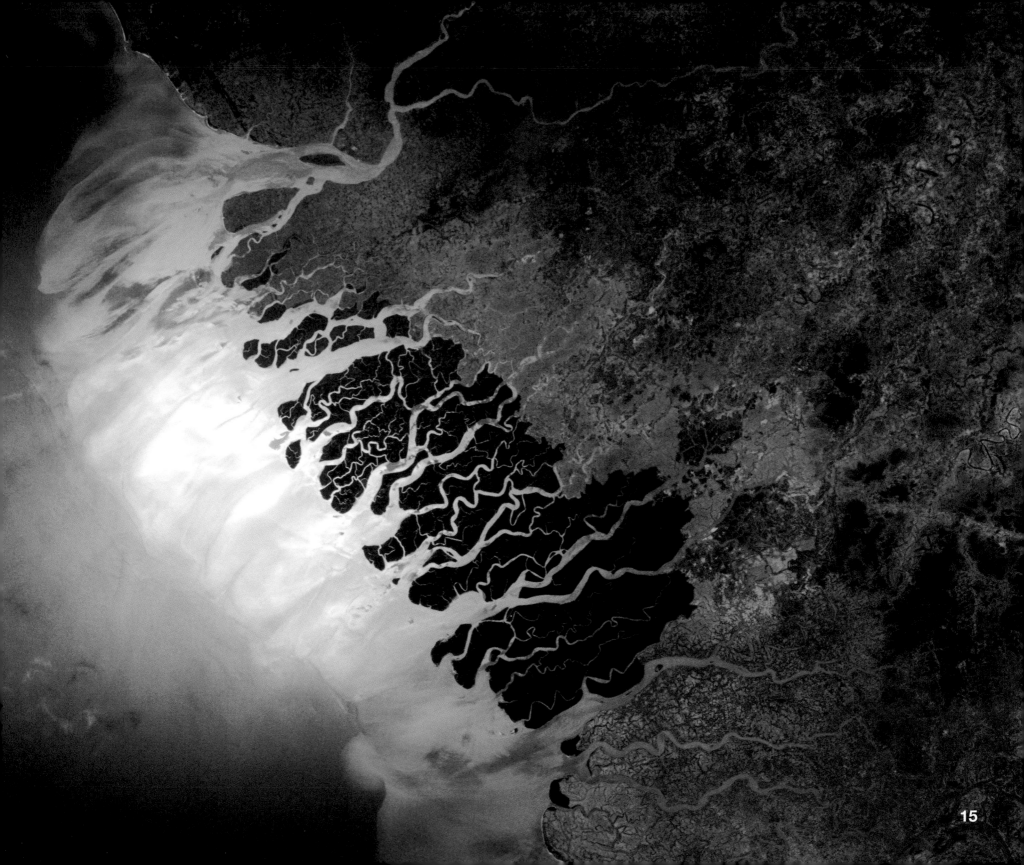

The Mississippi River Delta
is a bird's foot delta.
Each year, at least 6,000 ships
pass through this delta
to the Mississippi River.

People and Deltas

Delta soil is rich in nutrients.

For thousands of years,

people have farmed

flat delta lands.

Small farming towns
turned into big cities.
Shanghai, China, is on the
Yangtze River Delta. More than
18 million people live there.

Glossary

clay—a kind of earth that can be shaped when wet

coast—land next to an ocean or a sea

mouth—a place where a river flows into another body of water, such as a lake or an ocean

nutrient—something that people, plants, and animals need to stay healthy

sediment—tiny pieces of rock, such as clay, silt, or sand, carried to a place by wind or water

silt—tiny pieces of soil carried by water that settle at the bottom of rivers, lakes, or oceans

Read More

Hutmacher, Kimberly. *Islands.* Natural Wonders. Mankato, Minn.: Capstone Press, 2011.

Sidjanski, Brigitte. *The River.* New York: Minedition, 2008.

Internet Sites

FactHound offers a safe, fun way to find Internet sites related to this book. All of the sites on FactHound have been researched by our staff.

Here's all you do:

Visit *www.facthound.com*

Type in this code: 9781429653220

Super-cool stuff!

Check out projects, games and lots more at
www.capstonekids.com

Index

Word Count: 202
Grade: 1
Early-Intervention Level: 22